An
ILLUSTRATED
HISTORY
of

THE LONDON, MIDLAND
& SCOTTISH RAILWAY

By the same author:

LMS Miscellany (Vols I-III)
LMS Road Vehicles

An
ILLUSTRATED
HISTORY
of

THE LONDON, MIDLAND
& SCOTTISH RAILWAY

H.N. Twells

B.T. Batsford Ltd, London

First published 1986
© H.N. Twells 1986

ISBN 0 7134 4433 9

Printed in Great Britain
by Anchor Brendon Ltd,
Tiptree, Essex
for the publishers,
B T Batsford Ltd,
4 Fitzhardinge Street,
London, W1H 0AH

INTRODUCTION AND ACKNOWLEDGEMENTS

The London, Midland & Scottish Railway Company has long since passed into the annals of railway history, but its principal activity – running trains – has been well recorded by photographers for the future.

The L.M.S. was in being for 25 years (1923-1947) and there are still many thousands of enthusiasts whose memories of the company sparkle at the sight of previously unpublished photographs. It is the collection of photographs in this volume, many of which show some of the railway company's other activities, which it is hoped will re-kindle further memories of this once great company, and inspire the younger generations to continue their interest in railway history.

I have been fortunate in being able to use photographs from various collections, and in this respect I would wish to place on record my thanks to those individuals and organisations listed in the photographic credits, with particular thanks to W.T. Stubbs, G. Coltas, H.C. Casserley, V. Forster, V.R. Anderson, W. Camwell, G.K. Fox, the late A.G. Ellis, M.L. Knighton and the Keeper of the National Railway Museum, York.

My hope is that, through this volume, the broad pattern of the London, Midland & Scottish Railway Company's activities has been set out, and that further interest will be created for others, particularly those who seek additional detail in photographs to enable accurate models of the prototypes to be made.

A BRIEF HISTORY

The Years 1921 and 1923 are interrelated in the history of British railways: the first saw the successful passage through Parliament of the Railways Act 1921, which provided the framework for the grouping of the many railway companies into four large operating groups, and the birth of which became reality on the first day of 1923. The largest of these groups was the London Midland & Scottish Railway Company. That the Caledonian Railway nominally retained its independence for six months into the year is perhaps befitting the largest of the Company's constituents north of the border. The full title was quickly abbreviated to initials – L.M.S. – by which the Company has usually been known ever since.

BEFORE THE GROUPING

The major railways had been profitable concerns prior to the outbreak of war in 1914, and for the war effort they had been under centralised control of a Railway Executive Committee. There had to be coordinated effort during the war years and this inevitably led to maximum use of available resources. Control of the railways after the war did not immediately revert to the owning companies, in

---

◄ **1** Advertising was an important aspect of railway service support and slogans were part of the language. The L.M.S. perpetuated the old Midland Railway slogan, 'The Best Way', having more than a passing claim to this title with its high standard coaching stock. This poster was used on stations and in appointed travel agencies who carried tickets.

2 A map of the United Kingdom showing the L.M.S. dominance through the ➤ Midlands, up the west coast and throughout Scotland, with the narrow lines of the other three major railways appearing as though they were branch lines.

---

fact not until 1921, but several ways of unifying the railway system were examined before the 1921 Act was brought before Parliament. One proposal embodied in a Parliamentary White Paper in June 1920 proposed seven distinct groups, and what eventually materialised as the L.M. & S.R. would have been broadly divided: the North Western in England and Wales, with the Scottish Railways constituting another distinct grouping. The railways were run down and in need of new equipment in many respects, and the sale of ex-War Department motor vehicles to all and sundry was taking place to add to the railways' problems. Local freight traffic, followed by passengers, were being weaned away by one-vehicle road entrepreneurs. However, we know that the L.M. & S.R. was the largest railway operating company in the world in 1923, taking in the broad avenue of lines radiating north-west from London, to the Scottish border, north Wales, the greater part of Scotland (including all the principal cities) as well as into south Wales jointly with the G.W.R., and linking with other companies' lines at places like Cambridge, York and Bristol.

THE CONSTITUENT COMPANIES

Each of the major constituent Companies had a distinct character, and it was not surprising that they were uneasy bedmates after the grouping. The London & North Western Railway – known as The Premier Line – had in fact taken over the Lancashire & Yorkshire Railway Company one year earlier, and since much of their territory had been intertwined, they fitted well together. Both were workmanlike railways with the greater part of their traffic within the heavily industrialised areas of England. The Midland Railway was also a large entity, and whilst it too served many of the industrialised areas, it also saw much traffic from the lighter industries in the east and north Midlands. The Midland Railways coined the phrase 'The Best Way', and indeed the quality of its passenger stock was ahead of the other constituents, in both presentation and comfort.

In Scotland the Caledonian Railway was the supreme line, and the Highland and the Glasgow & South Western Railways were much smaller. The Caledonian had the most direct line from Glasgow to the border, to link with

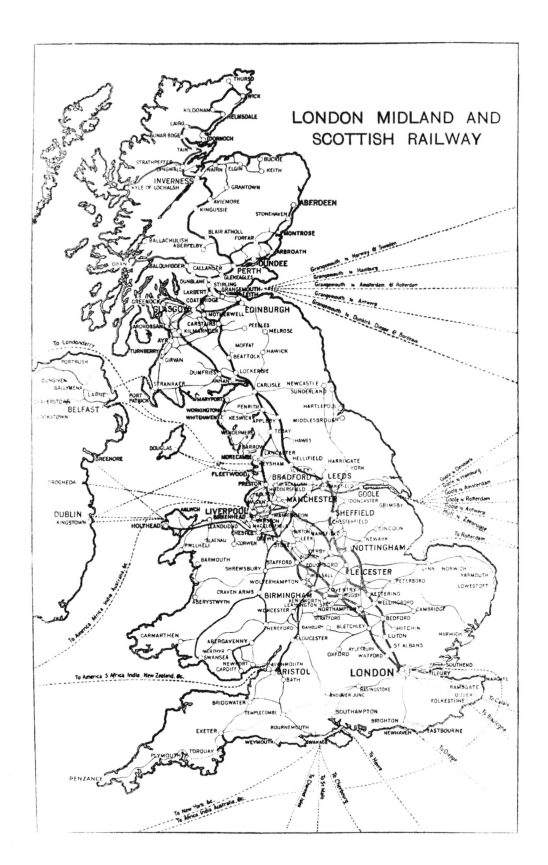

LONDON MIDLAND AND
SCOTTISH RAILWAY

the L. & N.W.R. and Midland lines at Carlisle, and hence the bulk of the traffic. It covered the central lowlands and up to Aberdeen on the east coast, Oban and Ballachulish on the western side. As the title implies, the area of operations for the Glasgow & South Western radiated to the Ayrshire coast, south towards the Wigtownshire Challoch Junction, where it met up with one of the smaller companies, Portpatrick & Wigtownshire Joint Railway, in which it had a shareholding together with the Caledonian, L. & N. W. R. and Midland. The principal G. & S.W. line from Glasgow was out through Kilmarnock and Dumfries to Carlisle and it handled much of the traffic to and from the Midland.

The Furness Railway could claim a route mileage of 158 miles with 25 per cent operated jointly with other companies, yet it served three of the English counties in what is now known as Cumbria. The North Staffordshire Railway Company was not so much larger than the Furness but it was more compact, centred on the Potteries, from which it drew the bulk of its traffic. There were also some smaller companies swallowed up in this huge one, yet the vigorously loyal employees of these small outfits saw to it that the standards they so proudly set were maintained for the new company. In all, 35 companies were merged to create the L.M. & S.R.

These smaller companies were entirely remote from the struggles centred on which of the two former major constituents would be seen to control the destiny of the new company. Since the purpose of the railway was to facilitate the movement of freight and passenger traffic, attention focused on future locomotive stock requirements. Crewe, and to a lesser extent Horwich (L. & Y.R.), had the larger express engines – 4-6-0s – and train loadings were often heavy for a single locomotive. The Midland at Derby had a smaller engine for its crack expresses, the Midland Compound 4-4-0s, and whilst loadings were generally lighter, it often resorted to adding pilot engines to ensure time was kept, even though the train weights were lower than on the old North Western lines.

NEW MANAGEMENT

Officials of the company, both at Board level and in senior management, had been brought from the pre-grouping companies, and were experienced in railway operations. Whilst the new formation had eliminated some of the traditional competition for traffic, the procedures to standardise systems within the company generated many new competitive forces. There was inevitable duplication, even after the initial efforts to standardise paperwork and procedures – indeed it would have been impossible to achieve uniformity in so large and diverse an organisation in so short a space of time, and many of the printed forms carried the new company lettering in pre-group company house print styles. In 1928 a more determined effort was made to eliminate duplication and waste, with the introduction of E.R.O. (Executive Record Office) references for paperwork, embracing forms, operating instructions, posters and the like.

Financially, the profitable pre-1914 position had been eroded during the war and in the immediate post-war years, and the railway companies were allocated £60,000,000 by the government to meet legitimate claims for compensation resulting from the use of their equipment during this period. These funds effectively restored financial stability to the grouped companies. The capital base of those companies forming the L.M. & S.R. at the end of 1922 was recorded as £526 million and, in exchange, the L.M.S. issued stock of close on £399 million; some pre-group stocks were exchanged at below par value. Even in modern-day terms the L.M.S. was a giant in purely financial terms, and in 1923 alone total income was in excess of £89 million, with total net receipts of £19,646,631.

It was in the stations and on the track that most people came to know the L.M.S, and whilst a widespread publicity campaign was designed to familiarise the company's name to the public, not a great deal was done to the rolling stock in 1923 to change the pre-group liveries. With 10,316 locomotives, 19,694 passenger carriages, 7,650 other coaching vehicles and 305,698 merchandise and mineral freight stock, to say nothing of the twenty thousand-odd road vehicles, it represented a prodigious task for the paint brush, even when spread over several years, and it is not surprising that some of the older vehicles never carried the new L.M.S. livery even by the time they came to be scrapped in the 1930s. What did matter from the new company's position was its image in the minds of the public, and efforts in this direction were not exactly assisted by the old company loyalties. The Board of Directors decided to appoint an outsider to take control of operations from January 1926, and Sir Josiah C. Stamp took office as President, with four Vice-Presidents, the Company Secretary, and the Chief Legal Adviser forming the Executive Committee. His was an exacting task, but progress towards the creation of a new railway image was made in the ensuing years, not least in the locomotive department, where a large new stud of express passenger engines began to arrive from an outside builder; I refer of course to the Royal Scot 4-6-0 engines. However, from the grouping new engines had been built, many to designs which owed nothing to Crewe, except for one 4-6-0 of pure L. & N.W.R. type from another outside supplier – 5845, the last Prince of Wales class built by Beardmore. George Hughes, formerly of the L. & Y.R., became the first L.M.S. Chief Mechanical Engineer and during his tenure in office 1923-5, the first new design of mixed traffic engine for widespread use throughout the system was prepared, although by the time the first engine emerged Hughes had retired and Fowler had made modifications to the original design proposals.

The livery for the new company was virtually that of the Midland, although some claim the two shades of crimson lake were different, the Midland lake having a richer, deeper appearance. Be that as it may, the new livery was applied to all passenger engines and coaching stock, whilst black was applied to freight engines, and goods stock had an intermediate shade of grey.

TRAMS AND BUSES

The L.M.S. had inherited two quite distinct tramway systems, an electric tramway from the Midland – the Burton & Ashby Light Railway – and a steam line from the L. & N.W.R. – the Wolverton & Stony Stratford Steam Tramway. Both were in a poor financial state and the Wolverton line never survived the 1926 General Strike. The Burton & Ashby closed in February 1927 after much effort had been put into popularising the line with joint rail and tramway excursions, but the growing numbers of local motor bus operators made the task too difficult. The L.M.S. had also become a road motor bus operator, albeit in a small way, with two services in the Harpenden and Tring areas, but the competition from motor buses for passengers was becoming more noticeable. To counter this threat the railway companies obtained in August 1928 an Act of Parliament which enabled them to enter the road motor bus field as owners, operators or participants with others. This they did, and from the time of this L.M.S. Road Transport Act the Company invested considerable monies in motor omnibuses, and the Derby Carriage and Wagon Works, renowned for its superb carriage building, began turning out omnibus bodies on Albion and Leyland chassis. Other investments followed in major bus companies and, not least, complete ownership of Crosville in North Wales and Cheshire for one year from 1929. L.M.S. participation continued until nationalisation in 1948, but direct bus ownerhsip ceased in the mid-1930s and the fleet dispersed to companies in which the L.M.S. had shareholdings.

The L.M.S. era fits well into three periods. Between inception and 1931 Sir Henry Fowler, Chief mechanical Engineer to follow George Hughes, brought in several new designs during the indigestion period when the new L.M.S. was settling down to a Derby-diet. Then from 1932 to the outbreak of war in 1939 a Great Western Railway engineer was invited to become Chief Mechanical Engineer and subsequently designed a range of locomotive types, culminating in the extremely graceful and powerful shape of the Streamlined Coronation Pacifics to head a new prestige high-speed service. Sir Josiah Stamp, later Lord Stamp of Shortlands, was slowly kocking the new company into better shape and William A. Stanier, later to be knighted and to become a Fellow of the Royal Society, was to give the L.M.S. locomotive department a new breed of engine types, the most noticeable and consistent feature being a tapered boiler barrel design to replace the characteristic parallel types.

THE WAR AND AFTER

The third period covers the war and post-war periods up to the end of 1947, when the L.M.S. and the other three companies were merged under the single identity of British Railways with effect from 1 January 1948. Nationalisation was imposed and there was no room for share value wrangles of the sort which accompanied the birth of the L.M.S. From 1940 the railway operated alongside its counterparts and the forces of competition were forgotten as the many thousands of railway employees worked around the clock to support the vital military effort to ensure victory for our forces.

Track maintenance standards had been considerably improved in the late 1920s and '30s in order to provide safe running for an increasing number of express trains. Average running speeds improved and so did punctuality, both important features when trying to sell the services to the public, particularly those who had to travel for business purposes. The ultimate in pre-war high-speed travel on the L.M.S. came with the introduction of the new Coronation Scot train in 1937, averaging just over 61 m.p.h., with much higher actual speeds on the fast stretches. Track standards inevitably dropped as the war period took its toll, and rolling stock too could not be maintained to the pre-war standards, either externally or inside the passenger stock. Movement of troops in specially chartered trains, vast quantities of armaments and necessary supplies were all handled and superimposed on an already intensive working timetable.

Parts for aircraft, guns, tanks as well as shell cases were made in the Company's workshops. New locomotive building continued after the outbreak of war and included thirteen additions to the Coronation or Duchess class Pacifics, nine of which were turned out in streamlined form. Even in 1940 the crimson and gold stripe livery adorned the five turned out, the remaining four streamliners carrying plain black.

With the war finished, Britain went to the polls and a Socialist administration was elected. That the preparation for nationalisation took two years is perhaps surprising, but the financial resources required to restore the railways to the immediate pre-war standards were not available from the private capital market, given that any return by way of interest or dividend was a prerequisite for risk capital.

Nevertheless, a new locomotive livery style was introduced in 1946, and although it was black with maroon and straw lining, it made a welcome change from the enforced grimy black of the wartime period.

Throughout the 25 year lifetime of the L.M.S. there was much which was either unknown or went unnoticed by the travelling public. Vast quantities of freight and livestock were moved consistently each year all around the system: well over 120 million tons per annum and more than 6½ million head of livestock. The trundling goods train was perhaps the one seen most often by the public, a public who were often given to grumbling when their express train was slowed and delayed through a goods train in front.

But what of the permanent fixtures of the railway scene? Station buildings, goods sheds, signal cabins and line-side huts were strung out along the routes and all were actively used. Apart from occasional repainting and re-lettering from the pre-grouping companies to L.M.S. style, few changes were made and the already old structures continued to serve and were passed on to B.R. ownership. However, it should be noted that some of these buildings were far from satisfactory during the winter period, with inadequate heating and poor gas lighting, conditions only alleviated for the passengers by the cheery words of the railway staff. Around two hundred thousand employees were given company uniforms, including heavy greatcoats, which for many staff were the principal means of keeping warm.

The L.M.S. slipped into British railway history, and 25 years later slipped away, leaving a railway scene which had already reached the pinnacle of achievement immediately prior to the Second World War.

THE PHOTOGRAPHS

3 The L.M.S. inheritance. The L.M. & S.R. constituted a most diverse collection of equipment on and off rail. Much of it lasted well into and even through the 25-year period of this great Company. April 1925, and this Precursor 4-4-0 is still in L. & N.W.R. livery, with brass number plate 1 and the name 'Clive', in Edge Hill shed yard. It was later renumbered 5253 before eventual withdrawal in October 1930.

4 One of the large Premier Line express engines, Claughton class 4-6-0 No. 2222, 'Sir Gilbert Claughton', awaiting departure from Euston Station, London. First opened in 1837 as the London terminus of the London and Birmingham Railway, Euston became part of the L. & N.W.R. in 1846. There was always an air of expectancy beneath the collection of train sheds which formed the terminus, and the principal L.M.S. express services radiated to Glasgow, Liverpool, Manchester, Holyhead and Birmingham. This engine was later re-numbered 5900 in 1925 when repainted in L.M.S crimson lake.

5 An example of the North Staffordshire Railway Company's rolling stock in the picturesque surroundings to Oakmoor Station on a Macclesfield to Uttoxeter train.

6 The Midland Railway small-engine policy necessitated double-heading the heavier trains, and here a 2-4-0 dating from the late 1870s is pilot to the 4-4-0 train engine – a Compound – and twelve clerestory carriages, on a stretch of what was regarded as the Midland main line to Bristol. (The London line was regarded as the secondary line). The M.R. bufferbeam lettering is in contrast to the previous photograph, where the engine number was carried in this position.

◄ 7 The largest constituent company in Scotland, the Caledonian Railway, had a number of 4-6-0 large engines; No. 916 shown here was one of the McIntosh 908 class built in 1906, and it was later renumbered 14617. These engines, and the better known Cardean 4-6-0s which were slightly larger, hauled express traffic between Glasgow and Carlisle until the Compounds and, later, the new Royal Scot engines replaced them. The livery shown here, a medium blue, was one of the most attractive of those from the pre-group companies, and a very similar shade was one of the early experimental liveries introduced by British Railways soon after nationalisation in 1948 for the heavy L.M.S. Pacific engines. The number plate is a casting, removed when repainted by the L.M.S.

8 The Glasgow & South Western Railway from Carlisle to Glasgow St. Enoch provided the Midland Railway with an extension of their services into Glasgow. A large Manson 4-6-0, even though it was one of only 17 such engines, is seen at the head of a rake of Midland clerestory carriages, the second and last vehicles being six-wheelers. This engine, No. 500 (later renumbered 14661) and its sisters continued to handle the St. Enoch – South and Stranraer traffic for several years into the L.M.S. period.

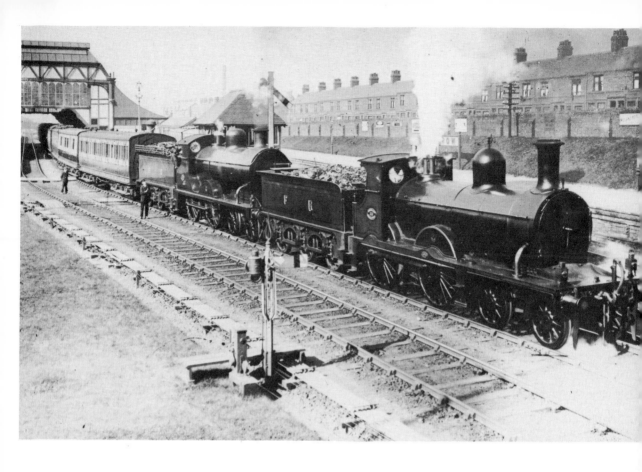

9 One of the smallest constituents, the Furness Railway with 158 route miles, passed onto the L.M.S. 136 locomotives. It was a small engine line, except for five 4-6-4 tank engines of large proportions. This view is included to give an indication of the rather smart Indian red engine livery and the two-tone carriages, set in the tidy surroundings of the Furness Railway's main station, Barrow-in-Furness.

10 The Highland Railway, smallest of the Scottish constituents with two engines, leading one No. 127 Loch Garry (14387) and a 4-6-0 Clan at the head of a mixed array of carriages. The leading vehicle is Caledonian, the next two Highland, a Pullman saloon, followed by two L. & N.W.R. and two more Highland vehicles. Highland carriage stock was one of the poorest at the grouping, and stock from the other English constituents, and much from the Midland, was allocated for use on the Highland.

11 In addition to the constituent Companies inherited by the L.M.S., there were several substantial shareholdings in other lines which were nevertheless important companies. One such company was the Midland & Great Northern Joint Railway which was another of the small companies. It ran to the north Norfolk coast, Norwich and Kings Lynn, and linked with the G.N. at Peterborough and the Midland at Little Bytham Junction, but provided through holiday routes from the Midlands. The L.M.S. had a half shareholding with the L.N.E.R.

13 Another of the smaller lines to come under the L.M.S. umbrella was the Stratford-on-Avon and Midland Junction Railway which, as its title indicates, was in the heart of some of the most beautiful English countryside. It was known as the Shakespeare Route and was a cross-country line linking with the Midland, L. & N.W.R., the Great Central (after 1923 the L.N.E.R.) and the Great Western. No. 17, later 2310, an 0-6-0 of Beyer Peacock, is seen here at Stratford on 11 March 1924.

12 Another such company was the Somerset and Dorset Joint Railway, in which the L.M.S. also had a half shareholding with the Southern Railway. Here new 0-6-0 Fowler engines, built originally by the Midland in 1922, are en-route to the joint line in 1922.

14 It was not long into 1923 before some interesting workings were seen. Given the rivalry, even bad feeling, between the Derby and Crewe factions, this picture is an interesting one. Former Midland 2P 4-4-0, still in full Midland passenger livery, was specifically allocated to Liverpool Edge Hill shed to work through from Liverpool Lime Street on the summer 1923 express to Cromer, Lowestoft and Yarmouth Beach, and this train, seen leaving Crewe, is formed of ex-L. & N.W.R. stock.

15 Passenger stations served communities large and small, and in many of the smaller locations they were the focal point of the village. The Station master was a man of some standing and experience and often lived at the station or in a railway house close by. Garve was built by the Highland Railway on a stretch of line between Dingwall and Kyle of Lochalsh, and in this view the station staff are posing in front of the house and station offices.

16 Another bleak and isolated station in Westmorland, Shap, on the main Euston to Glasgow line, which carried regular and heavy traffic. Most stations with two platforms were built with them opposite one another, but Shap had staggered platforms, as seen in this photograph. The signal cabin was on the platform. Passenger platform seats carried the station name in either a painted panel, or in screwed on letters.

17 The larger passenger stations were often covered over, and although glass roofs were provided in many, they soon became sooty from the constant barrage of smoke. At many stations connecting services with the other railway companies were made, and in this view of Chester General the brown and cream carriages of the Great Western Railway stand behind the L.M.S. engine.

19 Carnforth, junction of the Furness and L. & N.W.R., yet a relatively small township provided with a superb castle-like station structure. There are many interesting features to this station, and ornamental stonework abounds. The gable end stonework and the end sections of the roof ➤ sections were open to allow smoke to escape, and there is a rather odd telegraph wire attachment to the right-hand stone pillar.

18 A country station in the Derbyshire Peak District tidily maintained. The station garden has the slogan 'L.M.S. The Best Way' picked out in white stones and flowers. The station name board is a Midland flat board type. This station was on the line between Derby and Manchester Central.

20 One of the most famous places associated with the L.M. & S.R., Gleneagles, a former Caledonian Railway station on the line between Stirling and Perth. This station served the well-known Gleneagles Hotel, owned and operated by the L.M. & S.R.

21 Stations were large and the perimeter fences and walls provided excellent sites for boosting the Company's income from selling advertising space. In addition, this view of Bradford is typical of a city-centre station periphery. Lighting was through frequently-spaced gas lamps. Semaphore signals were used to control trains throughout the system, but smaller shunt signal arms were attached to the standard signals to facilitate station shunting activity. The track has an inner rail provided as a guard or check rail to ensure wheels could be guided around tight curves, and water supply columns are placed at the platform ends.

22 The L & N.W.R. used very tall signal posts to ensure approaching trains would have no difficulty picking out the main running line signals in places where buildings and bridges might otherwise obstruct the engine driver's view. Signal arms were provided at normal height with co-acting arms at the top of each post.

23 Signal cabins, or boxes, were greater in number than stations and goods sheds, and they provided accommodation for the men controlling the passage of trains through the use of semaphore signalling. Some were small buildings, but there were many larger ones and Preston No. 4 was one of the largest built by the L. &. N.W.R. The brick-built base housed the multiplicity of levers and bars in the locking frame, a complicated piece of equipment engineered to interlock the various moving parts to ensure the signals could only allow the passage of one train at a time on each section of line.

◄**24** Signal cabin interior with an example of the types of lever used to activate the signal arms, through the locking frame and wires or bars.

25 A smaller cabin built by the Furness Railway at Arnside, with a stone base and timber window framing. Each of the constituent companies had cabins which differed widely in structural design.

26 The Midland Railway also had a number of very large cabins and timber was used throughout in a sectionalised method of construction. This photograph shows the St. Pancras Junction cabin just outside the London terminus, with small roof ventilators above the two stove locations.

27 Vast areas of land were owned by the Company, with much of it in the major industrial areas, close to towns and cities. Here an extensive fan of sidings has been laid out to provide wagon storage and train assembly tracks in Stoke-on-Trent, with the main running lines to the left of the picture.

28 This panoramic view of the railway south of Alfreton shows the extent to which it encroached into otherwise unspoilt countryside. There are tracks beyond the four in view.

29 The L.M.S. emblem, 14 inches in diameter. A new emblem for the L.M.S. emerged in late 1923 to adorn the crimson lake carriages. It cannot be described as a coat of arms (only the L.N.E.R. had a true claim to this) but it has frequently been referred to as the emblem or crest. The centre feature represents the City of London, the two lower features being the English rose and the Scottish thistle, all on a bright orange base. Initially there was a gold surround and letters, changed in 1934 to chrome yellow, and then a pale straw after the war.

30 L.M.S locomotive policy was a central feature to the railway operation and it is appropriate at this stage to look at some of the early liveries applied to pre-group stock taken over. The first passenger engine livery, pure Midland style, was of crimson lake with the L.M.S. emblem replacing the Midland second armorial device. This photograph shows a typical Midland engine, Class 2P, used for semi-fast and branch passenger work, of a type which the L.M.S. later built a further 138 examples as a standard design, commencing in 1928.

31 This is a specially-posed train taken for publicity purposes. The engine is a former Midland 0-6-4T design finished in the first L.M.S. tank engine crimson livery, with small letters on the bunker side. The L.M.S. emblem later replaced these letters. The carriages are of the early period style with full outside beading and ornately lined in gold and black, marshalled to form an eleven coach non-corridor set for service on the Fenchurch St (London) to Southend service in late 1923. They were at the time a significant improvement over earlier stock and lavatories were provided.

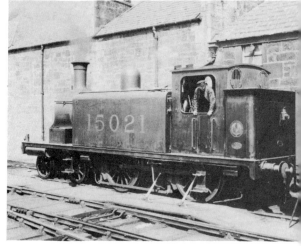

32 The large Midland-pattern numerals occupy a substantial part of the tank side area on this ex-Caledonian 4-4-0T seen shunting at Arbroath in 1930. The panels are crimson lined in gold, and the engine carries an L.M.S. building plate, a replacement for the composite number and building plate carried on Caledonian engines and removed after the grouping.

33 This shows the early black livery for freight engines with large numerals on the tender and a small red/gold-lined panel on the cab sidesheet. No. 3175 seen here in Toton shed yard.

34 One of the 1F special tanks from the L. & N.W.R. in black with smaller 14 inch numerals, seen alongside the south shed at Crewe, 1926.

35 Much of the semi-fast passenger work was hauled by the 4-4-2 tank engines, as shown here at the head of non-corridor stock at Scotforth, south of Carlisle. The carriages are of mixed origin bogie and four- and six-wheel stock. The engine carries its L. & N.W.R. cast number plate No. 1572, and livery, and the letters L.M.S. have merely been added in sans serif style to the pre-group livery.

36 No. 1117 is one of the compounds built by the L.M.S. in 1925, but it serves to illustrate the full passenger livery applied to the largest Midland engines which were almost identical to 1117. The engine is seen at Derby in 1926 after conversion to oil-burning, a measure authorised for a number of engines when it was feared the supply of coal would be seriously disrupted as a result of the miners' strike in 1926.

37 Another of the large Claughton engines used extensively on the Euston to Glasgow, Holyhead, and Manchester services in the early years of the L.M.S. A number of these were also moved to the former Midland lines working out of St. Pancras. The photograph shows 6018 carrying the name 'Private W. Wood, V.C.' in the 1928 livery style, with the company letters moved to the tender in 14 inch black shaded letters. The structure behind the engine is a coaling stage with the water storage tank above – a feature of L. & N.W. engine shed installations.

38 A diminuitive 0-4-0 Sentinel with lettering and numbering occupying virtually all the available side space. The letters are gold-shaded red with plain numerals, and No. 7163 is shown inside Lower Darwen shed, in 1935.

39 In 1936 a sans serif style of insignia was introduced with 14 inch letters and 10 inch numerals, with gold-shaded red, or plain gold. In this photograph No. 3726 has the shaded insignia and is shown on the turntable, in November 1938, between turns of duty. This was one of 935 engines of this class of 3Fs built for the Midland, and they outlasted the L.M.S. period.

40 Quite apart from the engines used in revenue-earning service, there were others which were in a service fleet, having been built specifically for use in workshops, or others which had been taken out of traffic and provided for the District Engineering Superintendent's use. These engines continued to carry London & North Western pattern cab-side panels, and this photograph shows 'Engineer Liverpool' awaiting the next turn of duty, at Edge Hill shed in 1932. Some of the Midland engines so allocated continued to carry the cast plate and the running number.

41   Engineering inspection saloons were specially built by the L. & N.W.R. (and Midland) for use with the Engineer locomotives. Although this photograph shows one of these special saloons after withdrawal by British Railways it is in remarkably good condition, and the long vertical panels above the waist and window style are typical of the L. & N.W.R. The engineer's special ran as required to allow the District Engineer to have easy access to all parts of his district, and the availability of his own locomotive ensured he was soon on his way when duty called.

42   Breakdown trains, comprising tool vans, powerful cranes and mess vans, were maintained at principal locomotive depots around the system and were manned by volunteer crews specially trained for recovery work. In the event of a mishap, one or more of these cranes would be called to the scene and work would continue around the clock until the tracks had been restored for normal use. The photograph shows a breakdown train on the Midland main line at Elstree, with a man riding in the seat provided on the crane itself, most probably keeping an eye on the boiler pressure.

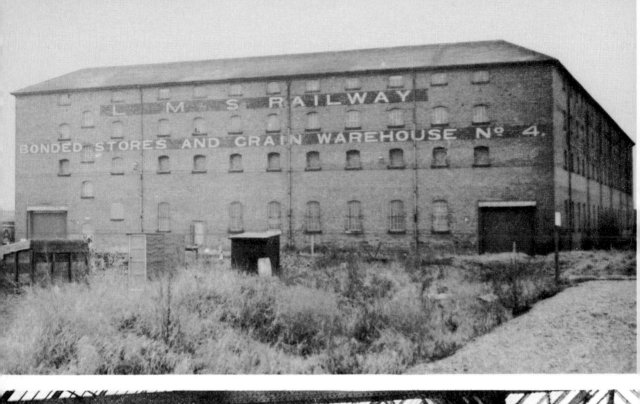

43 If it wasn't passenger traffic behind the engine then it was invariably freight, and the variety of goods carried was almost immeasurable. Warehouses were built to handle much of the traffic between road cartage and rail carriage and these varied considerably in size. For liquor traffic specially secure bonded storage was provided in the larger warehouses, and hydraulic hoists were used to facilitate movement of merchandise between floors, some capable of raising or lowering wagons complete with loads. This photograph shows a former Midland Railway bonded store and grain warehouse at Burton-on-Trent, and the fact that there were other substantial warehouses in that town is evidenced by the 'No. 4', which, along with the other lettering, was painted white on black-painted brick panel.

44 Inside the warehouse was a hive of activity as loads were either removed from or placed in wagons and vans, and this scene shows a variety of packages awaiting attention. Straw was used inside the wagons to pack fragile items or packages which could otherwise roll around during transit.

45 No. 1523, one of the Johnson Midland 0-4-0 saddle tank engines, shunting vans in the approach to a railway warehouse at Gloucester. These small engines were ideally suited for yard work, the short wheelbase allowing the engines to negotiate often tight radius curves safely, and the cost of running was relatively low.

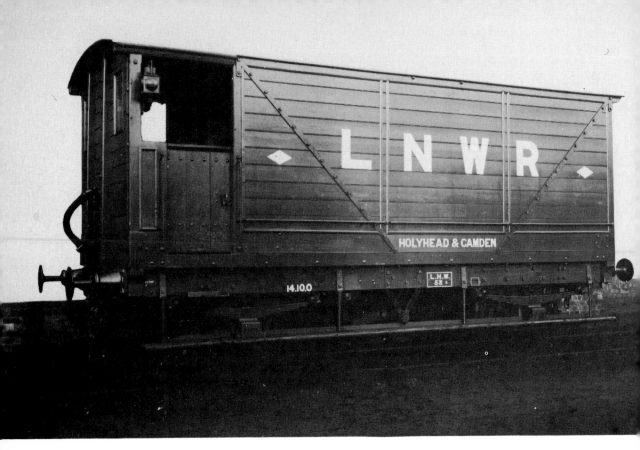

46 When the company was born it took over 305,698 wagons and vans, as well as providing running facilities for a colossal number of wagons owned by private organisations for which charges were levied by the railway company. It would be impossible to illustrate each type; there were countless standard types of wagon, not to mention the many special category vehicles. At the tail end of each freight train a brake van was attached and the third member of the train crew, the guard, was responsible for watching over the train throughout the journey. Coal stoves were provided in the van and a veranda allowed the guard to look out along the train when required. The wagon stock up to the mid-1930s carried large lettering to denote ownership, and the brake van shown in this photograph is also lettered for through working between Holyhead and Camden in London. Wagons also carried cast number plates, although the L.M.S. standardised on painting numbers on the sides of vehicles, which allowed easy recognition in goods yards, etc.

47 A wagon of one of the smaller jointly-owned companies, the M. & G.N., with shaded letters on the side.

48   Privately owned wagons were often gaudily painted, making the most of this opportunity for advertising. They were intended to work between the railhead used by the owner and, for example, particular collieries from which they drew their coal requirements, while some of the breweries operated covered vans for beer traffic. This photograph shows a black-liveried nine-plank wagon in Fox markings, a coal merchant in Derby.

49   Another private owner sector were the Co-operative Societies, who used painted wagons to obtain supplies of coal for delivery in their areas, particularly to those who were members of the societies. Some societies had but a very few, while others had sizeable fleets.

50 Wagon construction for company requirements continued in 1923, but it was the completion of pre-group orders rather than new construction authorised by the L.M.S. During the 25-year lifetime of the company more than 200,000 new vehicles were built, with an average of around 5,000 per year during the war years; 18,000 and then almost 20,000, were built in the years 1924 and 1925 respectively, and 1932 saw the smallest annual addition to stock in pre-war years, of 1,987 vehicles. Many of the wagons inherited from the pre-grouping companies were very old and unsuitable for intensive use, and this early building programme enabled many to be scrapped or written out of stock. Large numbers of early van bodies were removed from the underframes and sold to householders and farmers for a variety of uses, and it is testimony to the quality of the wood used that outside-framed bodies can still be found on farms. This 30-ton bogie bolster was one of 89 built in 1926 at the Wolverton Carriage and Wagon works.

51 Another early addition, a ventilated meat van built in 1927, also at Wolverton. Outside wagon building companies gained substantial contracts from the L.M.S. and etched in the annals of railway history are some of these names: Charles Roberts, Hurst Nelson, Gloucester Carriage and Wagon and Metro-Cammell, to name but a few. The builders used L.M.S. drawings, or designed vehicles which they then submitted to the Company for acceptance.

53 A Lancashire and Yorkshire express ➤
passenger design, 10446, nestling in the yard at
Newton Heath shed in 1931. Seventy of these
were built in total, with 10446 the first to be
turned out in what could be said to be full L.M.S.
livery. The earlier engines of the forty-one
actually built by the L.M.S. were outshopped
with their L. & Y.R. numbers rather than those
allocated by the new company.

52 New engine construction in the early years
was to pre-group company designs. This large
tank engine design was one of a class ordered by
the L. & N.W.R., but none were delivered until
the very early months of 1923. This engine, 7940,
was actually turned out with L.M.S. side tank
lettering and cast L. & N.W.R. number plate No.
468 and is here seen at Crewe South shed in 1937.

---

54 A 4F of Midland design, but equally an
unmistakable design of the L.M.S. One hundred
and ninety-two were constructed by the Midland,
and in 1924 the building of these engines
continued, with a further 575 engines being
added, the last being delivered in 1941. They were
solid workhorses which saw service in all parts of
the system, on both passenger and freight
working. Here 4057, a new engine, is standing at
Tamworth Low Level station in 1925, in plain ➤
black with the red initial panel on the side sheet.
The Midland and early L.M.S.-built 4Fs were
right-hand drive, but soon after 4057, the drive
changed to the left, easily recognised by the
vertical pipework over the front axle, and
reversing lever. These engines were highly
regarded by engine crews.

◄ **55** Another 1925 addition, built at St. Rollox works in Glasgow to a Pickersgill Caledonian outline, one of twenty.

◄ **56** Nasmyth, Wilson Locomotive Builders – a private builder-constructed ten of these class 2 tank engines to supplement the virtually identical ex-Caledonian engines used for banking express passenger trains over Beattock and other steeply graded lines. This is No. 15268 in St. Rollox-style 1927 livery.

57 Some locomotives could be seen pushing one or more carriages on secondary lines with the driver sitting in the end of the leading carriage driving the train through a series of cable links back to the engine. They were known as push-pull units, and here the branch train between Millersdale (on the Manchester to Derby line), and Buxton is travelling past Topley Pike signal cabin. Nameboards on Midland cabins were on the front, as here, but in 1935 instructions were given for boards to be fixed on the ends of cabins above the windows on all new installations, and this was later extended to the majority of cabins.

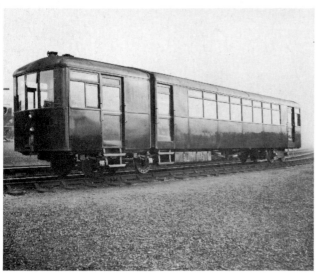

58 Another passenger vehicle was this Sentinel steam railmotor, one of 13 articulated units added in 1926/7 for use on smaller branch services.

59 The first new design of engine appeared in 1926, and although it had very definite Horwich, and therefore L. & Y.R., characteristics, the first engine was an L.M.S. product. The high running plate over the steeply-inclined cylinders and motion gave them a powerful looking front end, and it was inevitable that a nickname would be bestowed upon this class of engines within a very short time. The name 'Crab' lived on until the engines were withdrawn by British Railways some thirty-five years after building. They were efficient and fast-running mixed-traffic engines, frequently to be found on fitted freight trains and passenger excursion workings in all parts of the system. No. 13000 was the first engine and the livery here is works grey, fully lined for passenger class engines, and it later entered traffic in lined crimson lake. The tender was standard Midland design, and the tender footplate was much narrower than the cab footplate.

60 Another of the class seen here in the Belle Vue shed yard after re-numbering in 1934.

▼ 61 This shows one of the five engines fitted with Lentz rotary cam poppet valves in place of the Walschaerts valve gear, from new. The engine is in black livery with a single red line, with the 5P/4F classification above the number.

62 This view, taken on the steepest main line gradient, the Lickey Incline (1 in 37½) shows a 'Crab' supported in the rear by the 'Lickey Banker' engine, an 0-10-0 built specially for banking heavy trains up this stretch of the Midland line between Bristol and Birmingham.

63 The coal miners strike in 1926 caused the railway to place policemen on duty at certain locations to prevent damage to railway property. Here policemen stand guard at Agecroft shed.

64 Accidents were not a frequent happening when one considers the number of trains running every day in a complicated weave of routes. The prime reason for including this photograph is in fact to show the panelled construction of the early carriage stock, with extensive use of beading to cover the joins in panels. This vehicle, built in 1927, is of timber construction and the intact bodywork would indicate that this was a low speed mishap. The beading is black with gold edge lining.

65 Whilst the 'Crabs' seen earlier had been the first new design of L.M.S. engine, the Royal Scots heralded a new era in powerful locomotive design. There was an urgent requirement for a new L.M.S. engine capable of hauling the heaviest expresses without the need for a second engine, and the design stage was completed quickly after plans of the Southern Railway 'Lord Nelson' engines had been borrowed. There were changes to the Southern design, and when the first Royal Scot was delivered less than six months after the placement of the order with the North British locomotive works, the L.M.S. had found a new identity for its principal trains. Much has been written about the class and the way the 70 engines performed, but they were a class with charisma, even when modifications were made to improve visibility for the crew and they received side sheets alongside the smokebox, often referred to as 'blinkers'. One of the later engines, 6141, carrying the name 'Caledonian' is seen here at Derby, with small smoke deflectors on each side of the chimney. Nos 6150 to 6169 were built at Derby in 1930.

66 Another of the class in the paint shop inside
Crewe works, No. 6133, 'Vulcan'.

67 A nearside view of 'Novelty', No. 6127, in 1933, after the fitting of straight sided 'blinkers' and coal rails to the tender. The early names of the Royal Scots were later replaced with Regimental names and in some instances the matching crests. No. 6127 became 'Old Contemptibles' and the unique nameplate is seen in Figure 69.

*A*LL *locomotives, no matter how powerful and perfect, require periodical examination. The picture shows one of the "Royal Scot" class hoisted by a giant travelling crane in the London Midland and Scottish Railway Company's Crewe Works. The works cover 160 acres and employ over 8,000 persons.*

68 A handbook with the title *The Royal Scot and Her Forty-Nine Sister Engines* was produced for public consumption and carried interesting data on the new class of engines, and proved a popular title with the public. This photograph shows page 54 of this volume.

69 Three Royal Scot nameplates on display in the National Railway Museum at York. This Museum must rank as one of the finest and most comprehensive in the world, where much information on the L.M.S. and artifacts produced by the company are being preserved for future generations. (6127, 6110 and 6145 were the appropriate locomotives).

70　The year 1930, and further experiments with the second Derby engine, 6151, 'The Royal Horse Guardsman'. These sheets were later removed after tests for exhaust smoke and an early assessment for streamlining had been carried out.

71　The previous photograph and a number of others show engine shed scenes, yet none show a whole shed. This is the L. & Y.R. shed adjacent to the Barnsley station with a motor train in the platform.

72 Wemyss Bay loco facilities with water tank and turntable served by one track only. Engine depots were spread throughout the system to allow coal and water supplies to be replenished and minor repairs to be carried out without the need for an engine to return specially to the locomotive workshops.

73 The coaling stage with water tank above at Blackpool Central shed, with coal supplies arriving in the wagons, one of which is lettered 'Loco Coal', and both have the top doors open. The shed yards were always an attraction for railway-minded enthusiasts. Note the rather quaint smoke ventilators on the shed roof.

74 The largest locomotives owned by the Company were of course the articulated Beyer-Garratt engines, the first three being purchased in 1927. No. 4998 shown here was one of these, and this broadside view gives an excellent impression of the size of these machines. The three engines all had the fixed coal bunkers shown and later a single coal rail was added to prevent spillage. These engines had a characteristic clank as they travelled and they were used on coal trains down the Midland line to London from Toton and the shorter run through to Birmingham. The Garratt design was a Beyer-Peacock patented one, but the large boilers and other features were undoubtedly of Derby Midland extraction.

75 Long coal trains were the daily task for the Garratts and here 4999, the last of the initial three, churns along near Loughborough in July 1927.

76 This shows 4969, one of the later batch of thirty Garratts delivered in 1930 fitted with a rotating coal bunker, which was an improvement much appreciated by the firemen on these engines.

77 Electrification had been around for a number of years but there had been no widespread attempt to electrify, although it is on record that a special test run took place in June 1923 to assess the design of an electric express passenger engine, capable of hauling the heavy trains on the main line to Scotland. The test took place between Preston and Carlisle but nothing materialised, and one is left wondering why the company should use a pair of steam engines to obtain loading data specially, when such information was available en masse each day. The jointly owned line, the Manchester South Junction and Altrincham line (joint with the L.N.E.R.) was electrified in 1931, and the Wirral Railway in 1938. In 1928 a four-car electric train from the ex-L. & Y.R. Manchester to Bury line was modified into a diesel-electric traction train, but the experiment ended in 1929. The set is shown here.

78 The Midland had electrified the nine-and-a-half-mile stretch from Lancaster to Morecambe and Heysham, and one of the motor units heading two standard carriages is shown here in Lancaster Green Ayre station.

79 'Fury', No. 6399, an apt name for the high-pressure engine built by the North British Company in Glasgow in 1930. It blew up killing one of the crewmen only a few weeks after its first steaming and it was soon placed in Derby works and left. William Stanier had further tests undertaken after he joined the Company, but it was withdrawn without ever entering service, and a new engine was built using a new taper boiler and the frames, wheels and cab from this engine.

80 Another large and powerful design for hauling heavy mineral trains designed by Sir Henry Fowler, and again with Derby characteristics. Three were fitted with A.C.F.I. feed-water heaters and 9673, one of the three, is seen with the apparatus aloft at Rugby. This was one of the least successful of Fowler's designs and of the 175 built between 1929 and 1932, 61 engines were scrapped less than 20 years after building.

81 Some improvements to the L. & N.W.R. Claughtons had been attempted in the early period but they were still heavy on coal and maintenance. The arrival of the Royal Scots had eased the express passenger locomotive problems and they were successful engines, but there was still a requirement for a smaller type of engine which could be used over a wider spread of routes. Some of the Claughtons had received a larger and improved boiler and the Derby design staff decided to experiment with two Claughton engines by placing the larger boiler onto a Royal Scot-type chassis. The resultant engines were more than four tons lighter than the Royal Scots, and although labelled 'rebuilds', very little of the Claughtons were in these new engines. The first of these is shown here on the turntable at Nottingham. In 1934 the engine was renumbered 5500, and named 'Patriot' in 1937, to replace the former Claughton name 'Croxteth'. This view, taken on 26 November 1930, was soon after the engine reappeared and before the name had been affixed.

82 No. 5507, renumbered from 5936, was also nominally a rebuilt Claughton, but very little from the original engine survived. Smoke deflector sheets were added to these engines, and as they were not unlike the Royal Scots they were dubbed 'Baby Scots' by enthusiasts and railwaymen alike, although in later years they were 'Patriots' to many people.

83 Out of the public eye there were a number of works engines, some of which operated within the workshop buildings on narrow gauge trackwork. Rather surprisingly this Hudswell Clarke diesel mechanical was the first diesel locomotive on the L.M.S., arriving in 1930. An 18 inch gauge engine is seen here in the Horwich Works erecting shop in 1935.

84 A novel experiment was undertaken in 1931 when a conventional former Midland 0-6-0 tank engine was converted into a diesel hydraulic shunting engine. The original frames and wheels were used in the construction of this box-like diesel, seen here at Derby in 1935.

85 The operation of a railway company was a complicated affair, and whilst the Chief Mechanical Engineer would control the design of new rolling stock, there were teams of designers concerned with bringing the detail to the drawing board before the approval for building the various types could be given. Sir Henry Fowler is associated with the various parallel boiler barrel engines built, all of which have been referred to as Derby-type engines. Far from concentrating on the express engine requirement to the exclusion of everything else, some attention was paid to producing a small tank engine which could work in all parts of the railway, and have a capability of speed between frequent stop-start points; although they were in some ways a disappointment, the 2-6-2T of which 15527 here is one of the 1931 batch, they outlasted the L.M.S.

86 Small branch line services were not profitable and some were withdrawn in the more rural areas. An alternative to the usual branch train came in 1932 to the Stratford-on-Avon area, when a vehicle capable of running on normal town roads and also on rails was allocated for service trials to the town. The chassis was built as a road-railer by Karrier Motors of Huddersfield and an almost normal bus body was added by Cravens of Sheffield. After initial trials on the Harpenden to Hemel Hempstead branch, it was put into service, linking the L.M.S.-owned Welcombe Hotel in Stratford by road with the railway station, and by mechanically raising the road wheels it then ran on rail to Blisworth. Areas in the goods yard at both stations had been raised to enable the changeover to take place. A mishap a few months after entering service led to its withdrawal. The vehicle is shown here ready for rail running.

87 This small Sentinel 0-4-0, No. 7192, is shown shunting in Crewe South yard, a rather insignificant L.M.S. purchase.

88 The period 1929-1932 was an important one for the company. The shakedown from the pre-grouping practices had taken place and to improve the general image some new designs of coaching stock began to appear. The L.M.S. built a considerable number of carriages in the first few years and the so-called Period I styles, with window depths of 2 foot 9 inches, fully beaded and including a waist panel, were gradually superseded in 1929 by new and more sleek designs. These are commonly referred to as Period II designs, and deeper windows and the absence of a waist panel were the principal external differences. This corridor composite, with three First Class and four Third Class compartments is one of a batch built in 1931 at Wolverton; a further improvement had by this time been made with the absence of beading, and although the lining out follows the beaded pattern, the sides of the carriage are flush steel. The Period II style lasted until the end of 1932, whereupon the design changed again and the Period III from 1933 until nationalisation is generally referred to as Stanier's coach period.

LONDON MIDLAND AND SCOTTISH RAILWAY

NEW TRAINS

	SUNDAYS.	EACH WEEKDAY. SATS. EXCEPTED.	EACH WEEKDAY.
BIRMINGHAM N° ST. dep.	8·15 P.M.	3·15 P.M.	9·30 P.M.
LEICESTER arr.	9·45 P.M.	4·20 P.M.	10·40 P.M.

Ask for **WHITBREAD'S** LONDON STOUT & ALES

Ask for **WHITBREAD'S** LONDON STOUT & ALES

"CORONA" FRUIT DRINKS
4 LARGE BOTTLES IN CASE DELIVERED TO YOUR DOOR 1/-
OBTAINABLE EVERYWHERE, FROM MILFORD HAVEN TO THE MIDLANDS
FOR IMMEDIATE DELIVERY SEND A P.C. TO THE SOLE MANUFACTURERS
THOMAS & EVANS. L.TD.
KING'S N° TYSELEY

VIROL GROWING BOYS NEED IT

FOSTER CLARKS CREAM CUSTARD

FOSTER CLARKS CREAM CUSTARD

89   The public awareness of railway services was increased by street hoardings which often carried details of special excursions or new timetabled trains. This is outside New Street Station, Birmingham, in 1932.

90   The extent of the railway boundaries was marked by boundary posts, the majority of which were placed by the pre-group companies. The Midland used a piece of forged rail, as shown here.

91 The locomotives shown so far in this volume have all been in the condition in which the public would have seen them, but the construction process was a highly complicated one requiring the services of craftsmen skilled in a wide variety of trades. The major works were at Derby, Crewe, Horwich and St. Rollox. Here boilermakers are at work on a Royal Scot boiler; in the early stages of fitting out stays passed through the outer and inner steel firebox shells to create the cavity for the water, and the extent of this riveted construction can be seen in this photograph. The small and large diameter flue tubes are just behind the men.

92 A further section of a locomotive is shown here. The main frames, cylinders and footplating are partly assembled and at this stage there is much to be completed.

93 This photograph shows the same locomotive raised ready for wheeling. The boiler with smokebox riveted to the front end has been lagged and the outer sheeting added. ➤

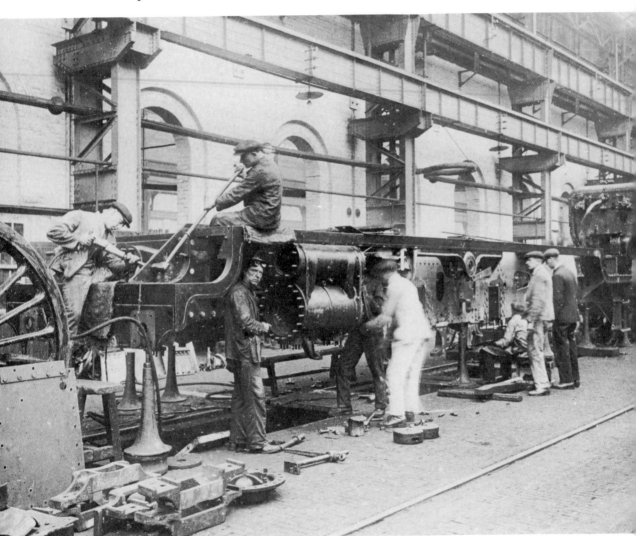

94 In 1933 the L.M.S. sent the Royal Scot engine and a representative train of carriages to the Chicago World Fair; before being exhibited it was taken on an extensive tour of North American railways. The previous three photographs show the engine during construction; this one shows the completed engine in fine condition prior to the tour, but it must be said that this was a one-off condition. The tour was an immense success for publicity purposes and in 1939 a streamlined Coronation engine and specially constructed train also visited America. ➤

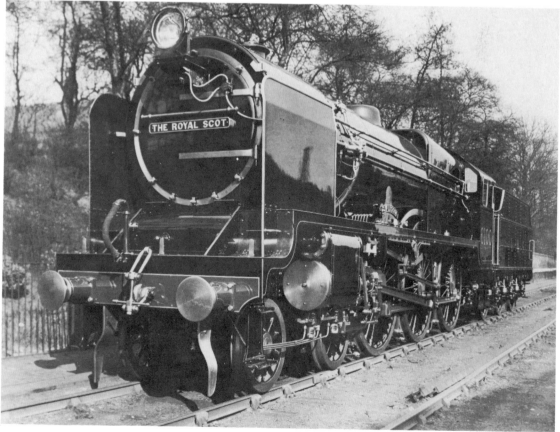

95   In addition to the construction of new engines, a great number of repairs were carried out on the locomotives which had been in service. This line of engines appear to be complete except for the wheels and motion; an everyday scene in the Derby works in 1931. A coordinated repair programme increased engine availability in traffic and cut repair costs.

96 In 1933 William Stanier was now Chief Mechanical Engineer. His experience was much needed and the first two designs which were built to his outline requirements were 40 2-6-2 mixed traffic engines, and two 4-6-2 Pacifics. The brief for the 2-6-0 was that they should have the power output of the earlier 'Crabs' and a Great Western Swindon-type taper boiler barrel; apart from some early modifications to the position of the safety valves, and the dome casing, there were relatively few other changes. The photograph shows the first of the class in works grey livery, but they were turned out in black, lined red. This picture was taken after a change of boiler and with safety valves in the normal L.M.S. position over the firebox crown.

97 Re-numbering of the 2-6-0s was done in 1934 and here an opposite side view of 2966 at Leamington Spa. Of interest too is the smooth ballasted track, the double slip just to the left of the tender, and the private owner coal wagons.

98 6200 the first Stanier Pacific built at Crewe in 1933. This and 6201 appeared 17 months after the new C.M.E. had taken up his duties and it was the most powerful engine on the L.M.S. at the time. It had entered traffic in works grey livery, and in this picture is shown in what the photographer recorded as a 'salmon pink', possibly an undercoat. It has the name plate blank above the centre driving wheel arch and was later to be named 'The Princess Royal'. Twelve in all were built to this design and throughout their time they handled the heaviest express workings out of Euston to the principal northern cities. They were a most graceful engine and were often referred to as 'graceful ladies', all carrying the names of members of The Royal Family.

99 The miles of track required regular maintenance and in addition to large quantities of rail, more than a million sleepers were renewed annually. Here a track re-laying gang is engaged in renewal at Berkhamsted, the old track sections being lifted out prior to clearing the ballast away and new sections relaid.

100 A train of hopper wagons is discharging ballast onto relaid track and the plough brake van is seen with leading plough lowered to spread the ballast evenly. Track maintenance improved and through better standards train speeds could be increased with safety. This trackwork is of the bullhead type, firmly held in the chairs with machined oak blocks (keys). The first experiments with the now familiar flat-bottomed rail were made on the L.M.S. in 1936, the change being one where the flat-bottomed rail was gripped to the sleeper.

101 Passenger Air Services were increasing, and with one eye on the potential competition this presented, the railways obtained Acts of Parliament to permit them to enter the field when necessary. In 1934 Railway Air Services Ltd was formed with the L.M.S. a participant; although the Great Western had already begun air services in 1933, the L.M.S. joined in and their first territory flight commenced between Croydon and the Isle of Man, calling at Castle Bromwich and Manchester. This route was later extended to Glasgow via Belfast. Services continued until the outbreak of war, and some services reopened for military requirements during the war. The Royal Mail contract was won for the first Air Mail service. Here a De havilland Dragon DH 84 is seen at Croydon alongside an Imperial Airways airliner.

102 One of Stanier's priorities was a mixed ➤ traffic engine capable of being used throughout the system on express passenger and freight as well as for intensive secondary and branch line use. The final 4-6-0 design was a two cylinder one with power rating of 5, and these engines, turned out in lined black, soon became known as the Black 5s. Here the first of the class to be delivered, 5020, is shown at Crewe soon after leaving Vulcan Foundry in 1934.

103 Much has been written about another new class introduced in 1934 which, though not dissimilar to the 5s, were regarded as express passenger engines with the same wheelbase as the Royal Scots and Patriots. The photograph shows 5620 in Crewe works yard when new and before the tender was added.

104 No. 5552, originally built as 5642, shown leaving Carlisle. Numbers were exchanged so that a new engine would carry the name 'Silver Jubilee' to commemorate the 1935 Jubilee celebrations of H.M. King George V and Queen Mary, and the class then became known as the Jubilee class. Altogether 191 were built and they saw service throughout the system, handling much of the heavy secondary passenger work.

105 Jubilee engine names on display at the ► National Railway Museum, Nos 5576, 5693, 5733, 5724 and 5629.

▼ **106** Two main types of tender were fitted to the Jubilees, the Fowler straight-sided type with coal rails as depicted here, and the Stanier curved top tender shown in Figure 104. No. 5701 is of the last batch of engines built and comparison with Figure 103 will show that 5701 has a longer firebox and a different saddle beneath the smokebox. All Jubilees later received the separate dome and top-feed boiler shown here.

107 The year 1935 saw the emergence of an experimental steam turbine Pacific, built in conjunction with Metropolitan Vickers, who supplied the turbine equipment. It was the most successful of turbine driven engines built for use in this country and was nicknamed 'Turbomotive', here seen at Camden in its early days. A number of later modifications were made as a result of faults developing in traffic but it worked well between Euston and Liverpool for long periods.

108 A typical L.M.S. express, with 14 carriages,
mostly of Stanier design, headed by 6207,
'Princess Arthur of Connaught', south of Crewe.

110 Despite being a heavy freight class they ➤ were initially turned out in a smart unlined black but their condition was generally grimy black. Note that these engines were not provided with vacuum brake piping when new, reflecting their requirement for unfitted work.

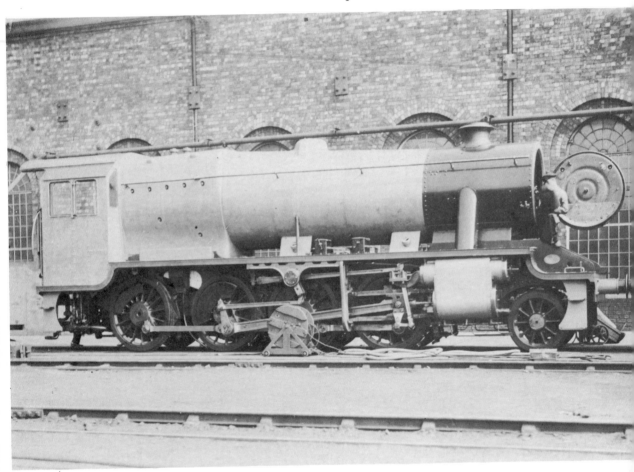

109 Final fitting out of No. 8000, the first of the Stanier 2-8-0 heavy freight engines, which also appeared in 1935. Here in works grey, they were built in considerable numbers and were used on heavy work in all areas. Many were built for the War Department and shipped overseas during the 1939-45 war. They had a characteristic 'clank' as they went about their work.

111 Stanier's version of the small Fowler class 3 ➤ tank engine, No. 73, at Newton Heath. A type used on short distance passenger trains, branch line work, and for banking duties.

112 & 113 show two types of container built by the L.M.S. to facilitate door-to-door traffic, using road transport to and from the railhead.

114 Two six-wheel milk vans were built in 1935, and 38551 was the second. The livery was plain crimson with the L.M.S. and number placing unusually reversed.

115 Most of the pre-group stations remained throughout the L.M.S. period and relatively few new stations were built. Those that were built reflected the then-modern styling and Upminster Bridge on the section between Upminster and Barking was one of the new stations in 1935. The shop front sections have still to be completed.

116 Cast concrete lamp posts, made by the company at its Newton Heath works, as were the platform edging slabs. The nameboard, although enamelled sheet, reflects the standard hawk's-eye style adopted by the L.M.S. as standard, with black lettering on yellow ground.

118 A large Stanier tank engine design which ➤ was basically an improved Fowler 2-6-4T type, having the same wheels and wheelbase arrangement but with tapered boiler and enclosed cab. They were a type suited for branch line and fast local passenger work, and were good performers in all parts of the system.

117 Much of the time engines were required to do no more than stand in the shed area. Youngsters at school, and others not-so-young, were always keen to visit the engine sheds, particularly at weekends when much of the freight traffic did not run and more engines were resting.

119 The Coventry Pneumatic Railcar Company ➤ built two railcars in 1936 with Michelin patented pneumatic railcar tyres, and with L.M.S. cooperation they were tested in the Leamington and Kenilworth areas. The driver position was above the main car level, as can be seen in this view near Kenilworth, but at the end of trials the L.M.S. did not buy the cars.

121 The bulk of the freight carried by horse road vehicle to and from the railhead was on flat drays or lurries of the type shown here. This was one of the first dray liveries applied by the L.M.S. and was one of the simplest. There were around eighteen thousand vehicles for horses, some of a specialist nature, but by far the largest number were drays.

120 In addition to rail services the L.M.S. operated a large fleet of horse-drawn road vehicles and there were more than nine thousand horses to pull them. Parcels vans were used for collection and delivery in towns and cities and this van is typical of many in company service.

122 A wartime picture of the faithful horse harnessed to the last type of parcels van to be built by the L.M.S. loading alongside a Morris commercial road motor parcels van. Despite road motor transport the horse stock maintained an important role in bringing and delivering freight for movement by rail. The white vehicle markings were a wartime feature.

123 Taking shape, the one entirely new shape of locomotive designed by Stanier to inaugurate a new high-speed service between Euston and Glasgow Central, the Coronation Scots. The class took its name from the Coronation of King George VI and Queen Elizabeth in 1937, the year the trains were introduced. Not only does this view show the outline but also some of the streamlining technique applied to give a sleek and efficient machine. These engines were an improvement over the Princess Royal Pacifics already in traffic.

124 The first three Coronation streamliners resplendent in their new blue and silver stripe livery standing outside the paint shop in Crewe Works yard before entering service. No. 6220 'Coronation' with a crown above the nameplate on the right, and Nos. 6221 'Queen Elizabeth' and 6222 'Queen Mary' alongside.

125 For the new Coronation Scot service three train sets were made up from standard Stanier-type carriages with modification evident on the roof to provide air conditioning, and of course the blue and silver stripe livery.

126 No. 6221, 'Queen Elizabeth', hurtling north through Hest Bank station on one of the early trips of this prestigious train. The first five streamliners were blue and silver, while the remaining batches were finished in maroon with gold stripes. Passengers were provided with a special route booklet and book matches.

127 After ten streamlined engines, Stanier brought out five traditional-looking engines, identical in size and performance, but with a round-topped smoke box and squared footplate front ends, and here the second one, 6231 'Duchess of Atholl', is shown in grimy condition awaiting its next turn at Polmadie shed in Glasgow.

128 Rather forlorn in black, with no trace of the sleek maroon and gold livery, 6226 'Duchess of Norfolk' in Crewe works yard. This engine was one of the last to carry streamlining, but the need for easy maintenance rather than fast running after the war led to removal of the panelling.

129 Parcels traffic was a source of much revenue and full-brake vans to run with passenger trains allowed a greater area of space for small parcels and mail bag traffic to be moved quickly. Although this vehicle is in panelled livery, it is a flush-sided period I steel bodied van to match the panelled period I carriage stock.

130 It is not possible to include examples of the many different types of coaching stock built by the company, but some of those which the travelling public would have easily recognised are included in the following photographs. This one shows a period III Stanier diner, 69 ft in length and with six-wheel bogies to give a smoother ride. The opaque window section was the kitchen area and normally a First Class open vestibule coach would be coupled to the kitchen end.

131 Sleeping cars were usually well out of sight when most travellers took to the trains. Evening departures and early morning arrivals were the pattern for the overnight sleeping car trains and train speeds were leisurely to give passengers the best chance of a good night's sleep. Another period III Stanier vehicle.

132 Non-corridor stock had doors on both sides, with compartments seating twelve Third Class and eight First Class passengers. This stock was used on surburban commuter services, branch lines and some excursions on short journeys, with the majority as Third Class accommodation. This eight-compartment car, all First Class, was one of four built in 1938.

133 Another full-brake steel bodied van. There is very little to distinguish this period III vehicle from the period I van in Figure 129. The livery is the final L.M.S. simple livery applied from 1934 onwards, but note that the L.M.S. crest was not applied to full brakes.

134 A sorry sight. Coventry on 14 November 1940 after overnight bombing. The wooden-bodied panelled stock has been blown to pieces; about half of the period III steel coach behind the engine appears to be intact.

135 Devastation at Manchester Exchange a few days before Christmas 1940, a scene which, with the previous photograph, illustrates the danger and difficulties through which a vast army of railwaymen, as well as private citizens, fought the dark days of wartime.

136 Some of the early carriage stock was converted into ward cars, pharmacy and theatre cars to form ambulance trains for use during the war period. A red cross on a white panel was also painted on the roof to be visible from the air.

137 Crowded trains, luggage and kit-bags en masse were very much the scene during the war, and the railways were a major support force to the armed forces, running special trains daily to move men and equipment around the country.

138 The Royal Scot engines were worked hard but Stanier sought further improvements, and even though he had taken up a wartime appointment No. 6103 was rebuilt with a Stanier taper boiler which took away some of the heavy front-end appearance of the original Scots. Here 6135 is seen on a Euston-Liverpool express after rebuilding.

139 Sixteen carriages behind be-grimed 6247 ➤ 'City of Liverpool' typifies the wartime express. Although streamlined, this engine was delivered in plain black livery, the sleek stripes from a bygone era but a memory.

140   H.G. Ivatt was the final Chief Mechanical Engineer of the L.M.S. and he introduced three new standard designs during his reign from 1946 through to nationalisation. This Class 2 2-6-0 6400 was the first of 20 such engines. Although in works grey in this photograph they were plain black with the 1946 lettering in pale straw, with the inset lining in maroon.

141 Locomotive cabs varied in complexity with the size of engine, but this illustration of 6400 gives a good impression of a well-ordered array of gauges and fittings.

142 An innovation for a tender engine was a rear cab screen to give greater protection to the engine crew when the engine was required to run tender first, a necessity when in use on branch and similar lines when the engine could not easily be turned round.

143 & 144   H.G. Ivatt also designed a larger
Class 4 2-6-0 tender engine and this artist's
impression in Figure 143 should be compared
with the actual locomotive shown in the following
photograph. The taper boiler so characteristic of
the Stanier era was retained and the eventual high
running plate provided easy access for
maintenance. All L.M.S. locomotives had 40,000
added to their L.M.S. running numbers on
nationalisation. The first locomotive is shown at
Carlisle Kingmoor Depot as 43000.

145   The future shape of locomotives – the first
diesel electric express locomotive built almost as
an L.M.S. finale in the final months of 1947. A
sister engine was delivered in the first few weeks
of British Railways.

146 The Royal Scot train passing Berkhamsted hauled by 6230, 'Duchess of Buccleuch', in March 1948 – everything L.M.S. except for the new lettering on the tender, and so a mixture of liveries was in evidence for several years after nationalisation. These engines, previously in maroon, and in black post-war, were the mainstay of the west coast main line expresses until the demise of steam.

147 Anonymity in Derby works yard, September 1948. Returned from war service No. 7607 became 47607 after overhaul. Note the French inscription and the broken buffer-head.

148 A grounded six-wheel saloon body of Midland origin, resting near Derby station in 1958. There is also a pair of coach bodies with roof built over in the background on the right. Grounded bodies still serve farmers and allotment holders today, testimony to the quality wood from which they were made.

149 The L.M.S., all but a memory. Future generations must thank today's preservationists for saving at least some examples of the L.M.S. locomotive types, and these can be seen periodically moving between the various steam centres scattered around the country. Here a Midland 4-2-2 leads the first L.M.S. 4F, 4027 and a Somerset & Dorset 2-8-0 on a journey to the Liverpool-Manchester 150th anniversary in 1980.

150 Model railway enthusiasts take great care to build accurate scale models, and in this miniature world the L.M.S. will live on.

PHOTOGRAPHIC ACKNOWLEDGEMENTS

V.R. Anderson: 23, 137; Author's collection: 2, 7, 15, 22, 24, 29, 43, 44, 47, 48, 49, 55, 64, 69, 86, 102, 104, 105, 108, 109, 110, 112, 113, 117, 120, 122, 150; British Aerospace: 101; British Railways: 26, 46, 50, 51, 58, 59, 61, 91, 92, 93, 94, 96, 114, 123, 124, 125, 129, 130, 131, 132, 133, 134, 135, 136, 140, 141, 142, 143, 145; M. Brooks collection: 68; W. Camwell: 71, 72; H.C. Casserley: 62, 77, 84, 99, 146; R. Cave: 149; G. Coltas: 17, 32, 37, 39, 40, 53, 66, 73, 79, 80, 95, 97, 98, 119, 126, 128, 139, 144; A.G. Ellis: 16, 20, 63, 127; R.J. Essery collection: 107; V. Forster collection & V. Forster: 3, 4, 8, 9, 14, 28, 33, 34, 35, 70, 78, 81, 83, 85, 87, 103, 106, 111; G.K. Fox: 25; D.L.F. Gilbert: 90; W.L. Good (courtesy W.T. Stubbs): 6, 12, 13, 36, 45, 52, 54, 56, 67, 74, 75, 76, 82, 118, 138, 147; T.G. Hepburn: 11; M.L. Knighton: 18, 31, 42, 57, 60; National Railway Museum: 1, 21, 27, 30, 88, 89, 100, 115, 116, 121; H.B. Oliver collection (courtesy V. Forster): 5; W. Potter: 38, 65; F.W. Shuttleworth: 41, 148; S.L.S. (courtesy P. Tatlow): 10; H.G. Tidey (courtesy V. Forster): 19.